Chest and the King

Written by Richard O'Neill and Michelle Russell

Illustrated by Mitch Miller

Collins

Chester was all set for fun at the fair. He went up the steep stairs of the helter skelter.

He pushed off and zoomed down the twisting trail. He lifted his bright red boots into the air and picked up speed.

But when Chester landed, he got a fright.
The fair looked odd.

Chester spotted a banner with "Summer Fair 1211" painted on it.

He had travelled back to the year 1211!

Then Chester spotted a scarlet cloak. He looked up. A king and his three servants stood next to the helter skelter.

The king pointed at the fair. "I did not allow this on my land!" he complained.

It was clear that the king was cross. But Chester had a plan.

"Will you join me to see the fair?" Chester said to the king.

So, Chester and the king had fun at the fair.

They pulled a string to spin the green windmill.

They went on the swings. They felt like owls swooping in the air!

Sunlight glinted off the top of the helter skelter.
Sweet smells floated on the wind.
The king's frown vanished.

But the sun started to set. The fair had to end and travel to the next town.

The crowds looked disappointed.

"Will you let the fair return?" Chester said to the king.

The king agreed and gifted the town a charter.

"Now the fair can come back next year!" he explained.

Chester shook the king's hand, then scooted up the brown stairs of the helter skelter.

He was all set to zoom back to the right year!

Charter

An agreement to let a travelling fair come back to a town forever.

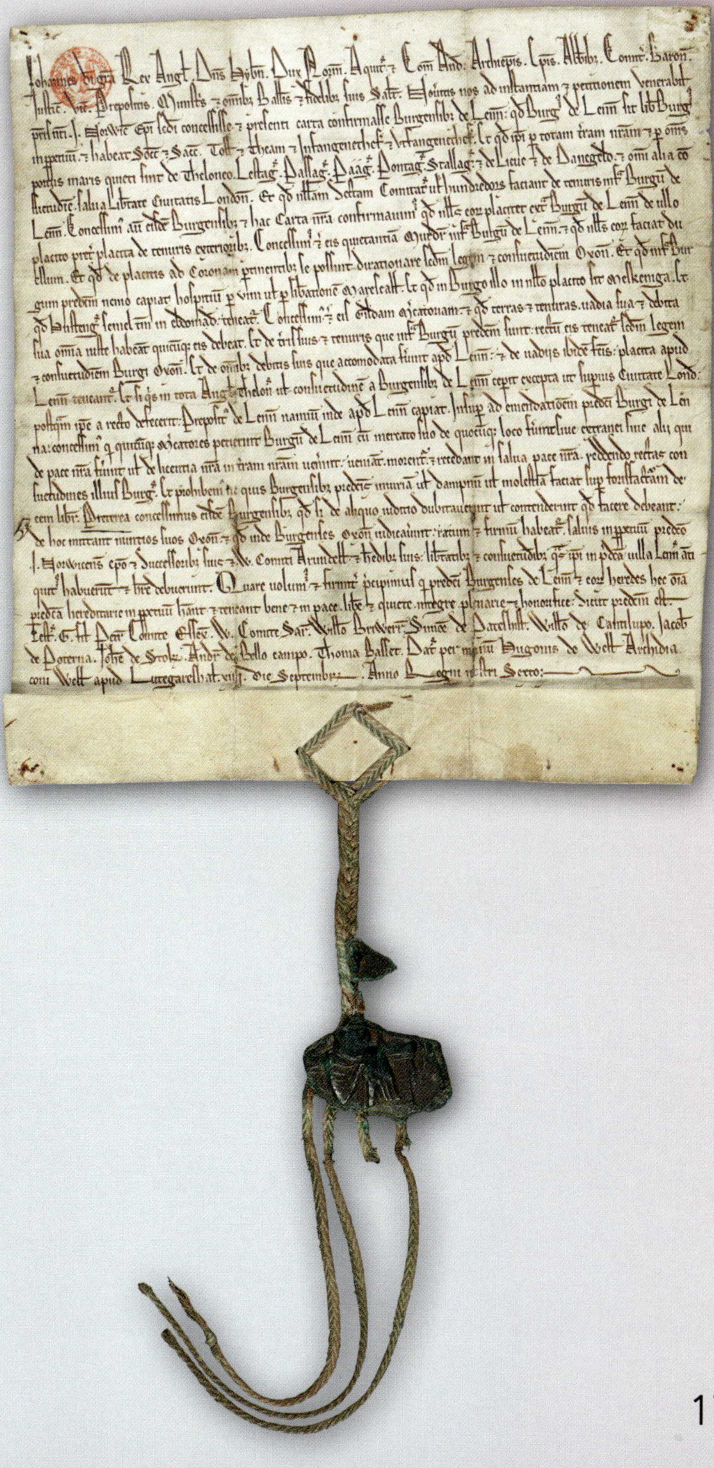

Charter fairs: Then ...

19

Charter fairs: ... Now!

21

Fun at the fair

Review: After reading

Use your assessment from hearing the children read to choose any words or tricky words that need additional practice.

Read 1: Decoding
- Ask the children to read and explain the following words as you read the pages, to check their understanding of the vocabulary.
  page 3: **twisting**   page 10: **swooping**   page 14: **gifted**
  page 5: **spotted**   page 11: **glinted**
- Point to **complained** on page 6, allowing the children to sound and blend out loud. Repeat for **disappointed** on page 12. Then turn to pages 14 and 15 and encourage the children to blend in their heads, silently, before reading the words aloud.
- Bonus material: Read page 16, then challenge the children to explain what a **charter** is to a younger child who might not know what an **agreement** is either. (e.g. *a written promise that the fair can come to the town every year or always*)

Read 2: Prosody
- Turn to pages 6 and 7 and focus on the dialogue.
  - On page 6, encourage the children to read the king's dialogue in a complaining and cross voice.
  - On page 7, ask the children to read Chester's words as if he was speaking to the king. Discuss how Chester might feel towards the king. (e.g. *respectful, nervous*) What is Chester's aim? (e.g. *to make the king less cross, to win him over*)
- Discuss the voice tone for each character – how can they make one sound older and the other younger?

Read 3: Comprehension
- Ask the children if they have ever been to a fair or would like to go to one. What are – or would be – their favourite rides? Why?
- Bonus material: Look at pages 18 to 21. Discuss how a modern-day fair might be the same or different to a fair in 1211. Ask the children: Which would you prefer to go to? Why?
- Turn to pages 22 and 23. Ask the children to retell the story, using the fairground picture as a prompt for what happened to Chester, and what the king enjoyed. Can the children include any feelings, sights, sounds or smells in their retelling?